Who Packed Your Parachute? Why Multiple Attempts on Assessments Matter

Quick Reads for Busy Educators

Cheryl Angst

Published by Cheryl Angst, 2023.

While every precaution has been taken in the preparation of this book, the publisher assumes no responsibility for errors or omissions, or for damages resulting from the use of the information contained herein.

WHO PACKED YOUR PARACHUTE? WHY MULTIPLE ATTEMPTS ON ASSESSMENTS MATTER

First edition. April 27, 2023.

Copyright © 2023 Cheryl Angst.

ISBN: 979-8223691228

Written by Cheryl Angst.

Also by Cheryl Angst

Quick Reads for Busy Educators

Gamifying Education - How to Engage and Motivate Students Through Games

Unlocking Gamification - Exploring the Impact and Importance in Education

Winning in the Classroom - Using Bartle's Gaming Styles to Empower Learners

Who Packed Your Parachute? Why Multiple Attempts on Assessments Matter

Table of Contents

Introduction..1

Limitations of Traditional Assessments 5

Unfairness of Traditional Assessments 8

Importance of Multiple Attempts 11

Multiple Attempts Help Students Learn 14

Multiple Attempts Promote Mastery 18

Multiple Attempts Benefit All Students 21

Implementing Multiple Attempts 24

Incorporating Multiple Attempts... 28

Ensuring Fairness and Validity 33

Potential Road Blocks... 36

Addressing Stakeholder Concerns 40

Examples in Practice... 43

Final Thoughts... 46

Call to Action 49

Resources and Tools 51

Further Reading 54

Introduction

THERE'S AN OLD ADAGE in education about the dangers of using averages as a measure of student learning. It goes something like this:

Three students were learning to pack parachutes. Student A (blue) did an excellent job on their first attempt, a decent job on their second attempt, but a poor job on their third attempt. Student B (orange) did a decent job on all three attempts. Student C (gray) did a poor job on their first attempt, a decent job on their second attempt, and an excellent job on their third attempt.

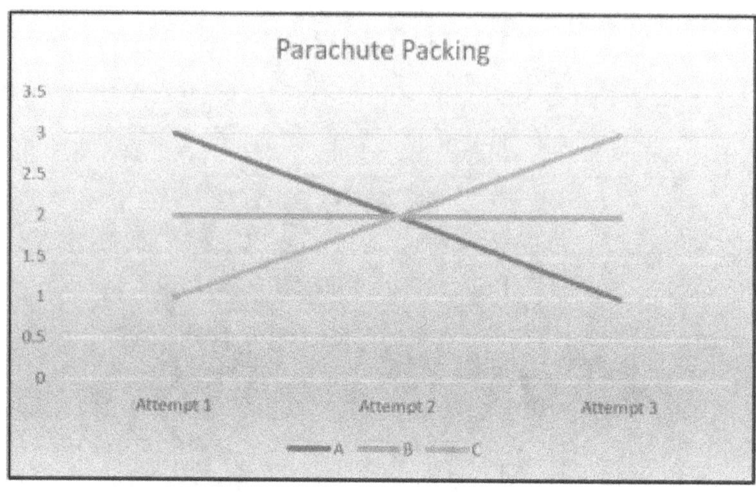

IF YOU WERE TO CALCULATE their average scores, all three students would have the same average score (decent), but if you had to jump out of the next plane, **which student would you trust to pack your parachute?**

Assessments are an integral part of the learning process. They provide a way to measure student knowledge and understanding, and they guide instructional decisions that improve student learning outcomes. However, traditional assessment methods have limitations that can not only be unfair to certain students but they fail to promote long-term retention and mastery. This is where multiple attempts can make a significant difference.

This book is a intended to be a quick and easy guide on the benefits of allowing students multiple attempts on assessments, how to implement multiple assessments into traditional teaching practicies, as well as how to overcome resistance to this approach. It provides a deep understanding of why multiple attempts are crucial for student learning and offers practical tips and examples of how to implement them in a fair and valid way.

The Flaw in Traditional Assessment

Traditional assessments, such as exams and quizzes, often have a one-shot approach that can be limiting for students. They may not adequately reflect students' knowledge and understanding, as students may have test anxiety or not understand the question format. This is particularly unfair for students who may struggle with the format of the assessment, but have the requisite knowledge and skills.

Benefits of Multiple Attempts

Multiple attempts can help address these limitations by providing students with additional opportunities to demonstrate their knowledge and understanding. This approach allows students to learn from their mistakes, reinforce their learning, and promote long-term retention and mastery. Multiple attempts benefit students of all skill levels and allow for differentiation based on student needs.

Implementing Multiple Attempts

Multiple attempts can be implemented in various types of assessments, including tests, projects, and essays. It is essential to ensure that assessments are fair, valid, and aligned with learning goals. This requires careful planning and consideration of the number of attempts, the time frame for attempts, and the grading system used.

Overcoming Resistance to Multiple Attempts

Resistance to multiple attempts may come from teachers, students, or parents who may see this approach as a way to lower standards or reduce the rigor of assessments. It is essential to address these concerns by providing evidence of the benefits of multiple attempts, showing how they can be implemented in a fair and valid way, and highlighting examples of successful implementation in real-life classrooms.

This book provides a guide on the benefits of allowing multiple attempts on student assessments. It explains how multiple attempts help students learn, provides examples of how they promote long-term retention and mastery, and offers practical tips on how to implement them in a fair and valid way. This book also addresses potential resistance to allowing multiple attempts and highlights successful implementation in classrooms. Ultimately, the goal of this book is to encourage all educators to implement multiple attempts in their assessments, as it has the potential to significantly improve student learning outcomes.

Limitations of Traditional Assessments

AS A STUDENT IN HIGH school, I vividly remember a biology exam that was particularly challenging. The questions were difficult and required detailed recall of information from the textbook. I studied for hours the night before the exam and felt confident in my understanding of the material.

When I received my grade, I was shocked to see that I had received a C-. I was devastated. I had never received a grade that low before, especially on a subject that I felt I had studied so thoroughly.

When I spoke to my teacher about the grade, she simply told me that I had not demonstrated mastery of the material on the exam. I knew that I had put in the effort to learn the material, but the traditional assessment did not accurately reflect my understanding.

Traditional assessment methods have been used in education for many years, and while they have their benefits, they also have limitations. One of the primary limitations of traditional assessment methods is their inability to measure a student's full understanding of a concept. Many traditional assessments only measure a student's ability to memorize and regurgitate information, rather than their ability to apply that information in real-world scenarios. This is especially true for assessments that rely heavily on multiple-choice questions, which may not adequately assess a student's critical thinking skills or ability to problem-solve.

Another limitation of traditional assessment methods is their potential to be biased or unfair to certain groups of students. For example, assessments that are only offered in one language or that require certain cultural knowledge may be more difficult for students who come from different backgrounds. Additionally, assessments that heavily rely on reading or writing may disadvantage students who struggle with those skills.

Traditional assessments also often only provide a snapshot of a student's understanding of a concept at a single point in time. This does not take into account the possibility of a student improving their understanding through continued learning and practice. As such, traditional assessments may not provide an accurate picture of a student's overall growth and development.

Another limitation of traditional assessments is their potential to create a stressful and high-pressure environment for students. This can lead to students feeling anxious or overwhelmed, which can negatively impact their performance on the assessment.

This is not to say that traditional assessment methods don't have their benefits. However, it is important to acknowledge they also have limitations. These limitations include their inability to measure a student's full understanding of a concept, their potential for bias, their limited snapshot of a student's understanding, and their potential to create a stressful environment for students. As educators, it is important to recognize these limitations and explore alternative assessment methods that can more accurately measure student growth and understanding.

Food For Thought

Why is it only valid if a student can demonstrate their understanding on the assigned exam date and time? What if they didn't get breakfast that morning? What if their parents fought the night before? What if spending three more days practicing the concept meant they finally understood it? What if the student is able to demonstrate their understanding the following week?

A common principle of teaching expressed by many ministries of education is that students learn at different rates and in different ways. As educators, we can agree this is true. So, why then, is taking an exam on a different date somehow considered cheating or unfair?

Unfairness of Traditional Assessments

I REMEMBER MY HIGH school Spanish class vividly. We had weekly quizzes that were timed, and we were only allowed to use pencil and paper to complete them. As someone who struggled with test anxiety and had a hard time memorizing vocabulary quickly, I always found myself struggling to finish within the time limit.

One week, our teacher decided to change things up and give an oral quiz instead. She went around the room and asked each student to answer a question in Spanish. I was nervous, but felt relieved that I didn't have to worry about writing quickly.

But then I realized that this type of assessment favored the students who were more confident in speaking Spanish and had better pronunciation. Despite having studied the same material, some students were able to showcase their understanding better than others simply because of the way the assessment was structured.

It was frustrating to feel like my understanding of the language wasn't accurately reflected in my grade, simply because I struggled with speaking in front of others. This experience made me realize that traditional assessments aren't always fair, and that there are other ways to evaluate students' understanding and mastery of a subject.

Traditional assessments are designed to measure students' understanding and proficiency in a subject area. However, the methods used to assess students can sometimes lead to unfair outcomes. In this chapter, we will explore how traditional assessments can be unfair to certain students.

One of the main ways that traditional assessments can be unfair is through the use of standardized tests. Standardized tests are designed to provide a consistent measure of students' knowledge and skills across different schools and districts. However, standardized tests often do not take into account the diverse backgrounds and experiences of students. This can lead to lower scores for students who come from disadvantaged backgrounds or who do not speak English as their first language.

Another way that traditional assessments can be unfair is through the use of timed tests. Timed tests can be challenging for students who have test anxiety or who struggle with reading or writing quickly. Students who are not able to complete the test within the allotted time may receive a lower score, even if they have a good understanding of the material.

Traditional assessments can also be unfair to students who have different learning styles. For example, students who are visual learners may struggle with written assessments, while students who are auditory learners may struggle with oral assessments. Traditional assessments often do not provide options for students to show their understanding in different ways, which can put certain students at a disadvantage.

Furthermore, traditional assessments can also be unfair to students who have different cultural backgrounds. Assessments that rely heavily on background knowledge or cultural references can put students who are not familiar with those concepts at a disadvantage. This can lead to lower scores and a lack of confidence in their abilities.

Food For Thought

Are we using assessments to generate a number in a gradebook, or are we trying to determine the breadth and depth of each student's understanding? If it's solely the former, then single-shot tests or other assessments are an efficient way of gathering data. If it's the latter (even if it's just a tiny part of the latter), then don't we owe it to our students to provide them with multiple opportunities to show their best learning?

Importance of Multiple Attempts

I VIVIDLY REMEMBER a time in high school when I studied for weeks to prepare for a math test. I felt confident and prepared, but when I received my grade, I was shocked to see a C staring back at me. I knew I understood the material, but I had struggled with some of the wording on the test questions, causing me to make mistakes. I went to my teacher and asked if I could retake the test, but was told that wasn't an option.

That experience stuck with me throughout my education and underscored the limitations of traditional assessments. The one-shot nature of the test didn't take into account the fact that I knew the material, but had trouble with the test format. It was unfair that my performance on one test had such a significant impact on my overall grade, especially when I knew I could do better with another opportunity.

As I pursued my own career in education, I made it a priority to offer multiple attempts on assessments for my students. I saw firsthand the benefits it had for their learning and growth. Students who initially struggled were able to learn from their mistakes and improve their understanding, while those who initially excelled were able to challenge themselves to reach an even higher level of mastery.

Through my own experience and the success I saw in my students, I realized the importance of allowing multiple attempts on assessments. It provides a fair and supportive environment for all learners to demonstrate their understanding and ultimately leads to greater academic success.

Assessment is a fundamental component of education that helps teachers evaluate their students' understanding and progress. Traditional assessment methods usually include standardized tests, quizzes, and exams that only allow students to demonstrate their understanding once. However, such methods have limitations and can be unfair to certain students. This chapter will explore the importance of multiple attempts in assessments and how it can benefit students.

Multiple attempts refer to giving students more than one chance to demonstrate their understanding of a concept or skill. This approach allows students to learn from their mistakes and make corrections to their work, improving their understanding and performance. Additionally, it provides opportunities for students to demonstrate their knowledge and skills in different ways, accommodating different learning styles.

One of the most significant benefits of multiple attempts is the improvement in long-term retention and mastery of skills. When students have the opportunity to practice and revise their work, they can internalize the concepts better, leading to deeper learning and improved retention. Furthermore, multiple attempts can benefit students of all skill levels, including those who may struggle with the material at first. This approach can help build confidence in these students and provide them with the support they need to succeed.

Another critical aspect of multiple attempts is its ability to reduce anxiety and stress associated with traditional assessments. Students can feel overwhelmed and anxious about having only one opportunity to demonstrate their knowledge and skills. However, multiple attempts can alleviate some of this pressure, allowing students to take risks and learn from their mistakes.

Moreover, multiple attempts can also help teachers evaluate their students more accurately. Rather than relying on a single assessment, teachers can assess their students' progress over time and provide targeted feedback and support.

Food For Thought

The notion of a review, or practice exam, is one way to provide multiple attempts that promotes long-term retention and mastery. Students see where their weaknesses are and can focus their studying on those areas or concepts. Practice exams also help reduce anxiety because students get to see the format and type of questions prior to the real assessment. Both the ability to focus their attention on areas for growth and gain familiarity with the structure and format of the assessment provide students with key tools for showing their best learning.

If practice tests or reviews are cheating or unfair, why are there practice tests for the MCAT, LSAT, and other high-stakes tests? If your family doctor was allowed to repeatedly practice for their admissions exam prior to being accepted to medical school, why shouldn't students be granted the same support for showing their learning?

Multiple Attempts Help Students Learn

AS A STUDENT, I ALWAYS struggled with math. No matter how hard I studied, I couldn't seem to get the hang of it. One day, my teacher announced that we would be taking a quiz on long division the following week. I panicked. I had never done well on any math quizzes before, and I didn't have much hope for this one.

But then my teacher surprised us. She explained that we would have three attempts to take the quiz, and that our highest score would count towards our grade. I couldn't believe it - I had never been given multiple attempts on a quiz before.

I spent the next few days studying and practicing long division, and I took the quiz for the first time. I didn't do as well as I had hoped, but I knew I had two more chances to improve my score. I went back to my notes and worked through more practice problems, and I took the quiz again. This time, I did a little better.

But it wasn't until my third attempt that everything finally clicked. I had made mistakes on my previous tries, but each time I learned from those mistakes and was able to improve. By the time I took the quiz for the third time, I felt confident and prepared. And when I got my score back, I was thrilled to see that I had earned an A.

Multiple attempts on assessments made all the difference for me. I was able to learn from my mistakes and improve each time instead of feeling discouraged by a low score on a one-shot assessment. It showed me that with enough effort and determination, I could succeed in math - and that has stayed with me to this day.

Assessment is an essential component of the learning process. Traditional assessment methods, however, have several limitations. Students are often assessed using high-stakes tests and quizzes that only allow a single attempt to demonstrate their understanding. This approach to assessment can be stressful for students and limit their ability to show what they truly know.

Research has shown that allowing multiple attempts at an assessment can provide many benefits for students. Multiple attempts help students learn by promoting long-term retention and mastery of the material. When students are given multiple opportunities to try again, they are able to correct their mistakes and improve their understanding of the material. This approach also reduces the pressure on students and creates a more positive and supportive learning environment.

The concept of multiple attempts aligns well with the idea of growth mindset. Students who embrace a growth mindset believe that their abilities and intelligence can be developed through dedication and hard work. By allowing multiple attempts, teachers can create an environment that encourages students to take risks and see challenges as opportunities for growth.

Multiple attempts also benefit students of all skill levels. For struggling students, multiple attempts provide additional opportunities to learn and demonstrate understanding. For advanced students, multiple attempts allow them to go deeper into the material and gain a more comprehensive understanding.

One important factor in the effectiveness of multiple attempts is the feedback that students receive. In order for multiple attempts to be successful, students need to receive feedback that is informative and specific. Feedback should highlight areas where students are doing well and identify areas where they need improvement. This approach helps students identify their strengths and weaknesses and focus their efforts on areas that need improvement.

We will delve deeper into the importance of feedback in a later chapter. Next, however, we will look at how multiple attempts promote mastery and long-term retention.

Food For Thought

Providing students with multiple attempts on tests allows us to also teach a valuable study strategy. Many students do not know how to properly review for an exam – they start at the beginning of their notes or chapter and work their way through to the end. A practice test (or first attempt at a test) becomes a powerful study aid if students are taught to look at the questions they struggled with or got wrong and then focus their studying on those areas. By providing students with multiple attempts, we not only provide them with opportunities to demonstrate better learning, we can also teach them how to become better students.

Multiple Attempts Promote Mastery

I REMEMBER STRUGGLING in my high school biology class. We had weekly quizzes, and I never seemed to do well on them. No matter how hard I studied, I always seemed to miss something or forget an important detail. It was frustrating because I knew I was putting in the effort, but my grades didn't reflect it.

One day, my teacher announced that she was going to start giving us multiple attempts on our quizzes. She explained that she wanted us to have the chance to learn from our mistakes and improve our understanding of the material. I was thrilled at the prospect of having another chance to do better.

The first time I took advantage of the multiple attempts, I was able to identify the areas where I struggled and focus on them. I retook the quiz, and I did much better. I continued to use this approach for the rest of the school year, and my grades started to improve. I felt like I was actually learning the material instead of just trying to memorize it for a quiz.

As the end of the year approached, I realized that I had a much better understanding of biology than I ever thought possible. I felt more confident in my abilities and proud of the progress I had made. Looking back, I know that the multiple attempts on our quizzes were the key to my success in that class. They gave me the chance to learn from my mistakes, identify my weaknesses, and improve my understanding of the material.

In the previous chapter, we discussed the importance of multiple attempts in helping students learn. In this chapter, we will explore some examples of how multiple attempts promote long-term retention and mastery.

One of the biggest benefits of multiple attempts is that it allows students to practice and review the material over a period of time, which is essential for long-term retention. When students are only given one chance to demonstrate their understanding, they may forget the material soon after the assessment is over. However, when students are given multiple attempts, they are able to revisit the material and reinforce their learning over time.

For example, let's say a student is struggling with a particular concept in math. In a traditional assessment, the student may receive a poor grade and move on to the next topic without fully understanding the concept. However, if the student is given multiple attempts to demonstrate their understanding, they can continue to practice and review the material until they fully grasp the concept. This type of repetition and reinforcement is crucial for long-term retention.

Multiple attempts can also help students achieve mastery in a subject. Mastery means more than just understanding a concept or completing a task; it means being able to apply that knowledge in different situations and contexts. When students are given multiple opportunities to practice and demonstrate their understanding, they are more likely to achieve mastery.

For example, let's say a student is learning a new language. If they are only given one opportunity to demonstrate their understanding, they may only be able to recall certain words or phrases in a specific context. However, if they are given multiple opportunities to practice and use the language in different situations, they are more likely to achieve mastery and be able to use the language in a variety of contexts.

Food For Thought

"Wall Math" has been around for more than a quarter century, and it came about when educators noticed students tended to learn a concept in math, get tested on it, and then promptly forget about it. It was common for students to claim, "We never learned that!" when their next year's teacher introduced a concept by tying it back to something from the previous year. "Wall Math" was a bulletin board in the classroom with 12-20 questions, each covering a different math concept (e.g., number concepts, fractions, algebra, geometry, integers, graphing data, etc.). Each week the questions changed. Students completed "Wall Math" as part of their weekly work in their math class and showed much better retention of all concepts the following year.

If repeated practice breeds long-term retention and mastery, then why are so many teachers reluctant to extend the same principle to their assessments?

Multiple Attempts Benefit All Students

AS A TEACHER, I OFTEN see my students struggle with traditional assessments that only allow for one attempt. I remember one student, in particular, who consistently struggled with multiple-choice tests. No matter how much we reviewed the material beforehand, he would still only score a C or lower on the first attempt.

But when I introduced multiple attempts on assessments, I saw a significant improvement in his performance. He was able to review his mistakes and learn from them, and on his second attempt, he scored a B. By the third attempt, he had mastered the material and earned an A.

What struck me was that this student wasn't necessarily less intelligent than his peers; he just needed more opportunities to demonstrate his understanding. Allowing multiple attempts gave him the chance to learn from his mistakes and improve, ultimately leading to his success.

Since then, I've made it a point to offer multiple attempts on assessments for all my students, regardless of their ability level. It has been rewarding to see how many of them have benefited from this approach, as they are able to demonstrate their understanding and improve their performance over time.

While multiple attempts are often associated with struggling students, they can also be a valuable tool for high-performing students who seek to achieve mastery.

Multiple Attempts Encourage Risk-Taking

Providing multiple attempts encourages students to take risks and attempt challenging tasks, knowing that they will have another opportunity to try again. This can benefit students of all skill levels, as it fosters a growth mindset and helps students to push beyond their comfort zones.

Multiple Attempts Provide Feedback

Each attempt provides valuable feedback to the student, allowing them to learn from their mistakes and make improvements. This iterative process can benefit all students, as it helps them to develop a deeper understanding of the material and identify areas where they need to improve.

Multiple Attempts Promote Mastery

For high-performing students, multiple attempts provide an opportunity to achieve true mastery of the material. By allowing them to continue refining their skills and knowledge, they can go beyond simply achieving a passing grade and truly excel in the subject matter.

Multiple Attempts Build Confidence

Providing multiple attempts can also help build confidence in students of all skill levels. By showing them that they are capable of improvement and growth, they can develop a sense of self-efficacy that will serve them well in future academic and professional endeavors.

Food For Thought

Providing multiple attempts for students of all skill levels can have numerous benefits, including encouraging risk-taking, providing valuable feedback, promoting mastery, and building confidence. If we value these benefits, then let's apply a strategy (multiple attempts) that naturally breeds them!

Implementing Multiple Attempts

AS A MIDDLE SCHOOL social studies teacher, I always felt that traditional assessments did not accurately measure my students' understanding of the material. So, I decided to implement multiple attempts on assessments to see if it would make a difference.

I started by creating a review sheet that covered the key concepts of the unit. I allowed my students to use the review sheet during their first attempt at the assessment. After they completed the assessment, I graded it and provided feedback on their performance. Then, I gave them the opportunity to retake the assessment with a different set of questions that still covered the same concepts.

To my surprise, the results were incredible. Students who had struggled on the initial assessment were able to use the feedback and their review sheet to improve on the retake. Those who had done well on the first attempt were challenged with new questions that tested their understanding on a deeper level.

What impressed me the most was the improvement of my struggling students. They were able to show me that they truly understood the material once they were given multiple chances to demonstrate their knowledge. I saw an increase in their confidence and engagement in class discussions as well.

Implementing multiple attempts on assessments in my classroom not only allowed my students to learn at their own pace, but it also gave them the opportunity to build their knowledge and understanding over time. It was a small change, but it had a big impact on the success of my students.

Assessments are an integral part of the learning process, and they help to measure the knowledge and understanding of students. However, traditional assessment methods that provide only one opportunity for students to demonstrate their learning can be limiting and can disadvantage some students. Multiple attempts for assessments offer a solution to this problem, providing students with more opportunities to show their understanding of the subject matter. In this chapter, we will discuss how to implement multiple attempts into assessments.

Importance of Clear Learning Objectives

To implement multiple attempts into assessments, it is important to first establish clear learning objectives. Learning objectives should be specific and measurable, outlining the intended outcomes of the assessment. This will help ensure that the assessment is fair and that students are able to focus their efforts on achieving the desired outcomes.

For example, if the learning objective is to describe the significance of events when placed in chronological order, then students should not lose marks for poor spelling or grammar (as their ability to spell has nothing to do with their ability to assess the significance of certain events).

Creating Multiple Versions of the Assessment

One way to implement multiple attempts into assessments is by creating multiple versions of the assessment. This can be done by altering the questions or by changing the format of the assessment. By creating multiple versions, students have the opportunity to learn from their mistakes and improve their understanding of the subject matter.

Educators often worry that students won't spend time learning the content when given a second attempt, but will focus their efforts on memorizing the answers to the questions they got wrong. Creating a second (or third, or fourth) version of an assessment eliminates the concern that students aren't truly learning the material. And, with technology currently available, it can be quite simple for educators to create multiple versions of their assessments.

Offering a Retake

Another way to implement multiple attempts into assessments is by offering a retake option. This provides students with the opportunity to review their mistakes and improve their understanding of the subject matter. However, it is important to establish clear guidelines for the retake option, such as a time limit or a limit on the number of retakes allowed.

A retake should be considered as valid as the original assessment. This means the scores on the first and second attemtps shouldn't be averaged. If the goal is to determine the student's best understanding, then the higher of the two scores should arguably be representative of that.

Establishing a Feedback System

To help students improve their understanding of the subject matter, it is important to establish a feedback system. This can be done by providing detailed feedback on their responses, highlighting areas for improvement and providing suggestions for further study. Additionally, students can be encouraged to seek feedback from their peers or from the teacher.

Implementing multiple attempts into assessments provides students with more opportunities to demonstrate their understanding of the subject matter. Clear learning objectives, creating multiple versions of the assessment, offering a retake option, and establishing a feedback system are all effective ways to implement multiple attempts into assessments. By doing so, we can help ensure that assessments are fair and that students are able to fully demonstrate their learning.

Incorporating Multiple Attempts

I HAVE ALWAYS BELIEVED that traditional assessments alone do not provide a complete picture of a student's learning. So, I decided to incorporate multiple attempts into my science assessments to help my students learn and improve their understanding.

I started by creating formative assessments that students could take multiple times until they mastered the content. For instance, I developed a set of questions on a particular topic, and students were allowed to retake the assessment if they did not score well on their first attempt. This approach allowed students to review the material and apply their understanding, leading to better performance in their subsequent attempts.

In addition, I also introduced open-ended projects that allowed students to showcase their creativity and apply their knowledge. I provided them with various options to choose from, such as designing an experiment or creating a model, and allowed them to work in groups or individually.

Through these assessments, my students had more opportunities to practice and learn from their mistakes, leading to higher retention and mastery of the material. I noticed that my students were more engaged and motivated to learn since they knew they had multiple chances to succeed.

Overall, incorporating multiple attempts into my assessments has been a successful addition to my teaching methodology. It has allowed me to provide a more comprehensive assessment of my students' understanding, while also encouraging them to take control of their learning and strive for mastery.

Multiple attempts can be incorporated into a wide range of assessment types to improve student learning outcomes. In this chapter, we will discuss different types of assessments that can benefit from allowing multiple attempts, and provide examples of how to implement this approach effectively.

Quizzes and Tests

Traditional quizzes and tests are one of the most common forms of assessment used in education. However, allowing only one attempt can put undue pressure on students, and the stress of the situation can negatively impact their performance. By allowing multiple attempts, students can take the time to reflect on their mistakes and learn from them.

For example, a teacher can create a quiz that has a set number of questions, but allows students to take the quiz multiple times until they achieve a specific grade. This approach gives students the opportunity to learn from their mistakes and correct them, resulting in better retention of the material.

Another option is to create multiple versions of the same test. Many Learning Management Systems (LMS) allow educators to create test banks within a quiz so that each time a student takes the assessment they are presented with different questions from the bank. This automation reduces teacher workload while providing students with multiple attempts to succeed at the assessment.

Writing Assignments

Writing assignments are another form of assessment that can benefit from multiple attempts. This approach is particularly useful for students who struggle with writing or language skills.

For example, a teacher can assign a writing assignment, and allow students to submit multiple drafts for feedback and revisions. This approach not only helps students improve their writing skills but also encourages them to reflect on their own learning process.

To reduce teacher workload, students could be given a block of time to engage in peer review where the feedback is given by a fellow student based on criteria listed by the teacher.

Presentations

Presentations are a form of assessment that requires both content knowledge and communication skills. Allowing multiple attempts for presentations can help students overcome performance anxiety and improve their public speaking skills.

For example, a teacher can assign a presentation and allow students to rehearse and practice multiple times before the final presentation. This approach helps students to identify areas that need improvement, and encourages them to take ownership of their learning process.

To reduce the in-class time required to watch multiple attempts at student presentations, educators can offer "retakes" for presentations, but the retake must be submitted as a video recording. This allows teachers to move forward with class content while still providing students with another chance to demonstrate their best learning.

Projects

Project-based assessments can take many different forms, such as group projects, research papers, or creative assignments. Allowing multiple attempts for project-based assessments can help students refine their ideas and improve their work over time.

For example, a teacher can assign a group project and allow multiple drafts or iterations of the project before the final submission. This approach encourages collaboration and provides opportunities for students to learn from their mistakes.

Projects are another form of assessment that benefit from peer review. Students, or student groups, provide feedback on another group's project based on criteria given by the teacher. This not only helps the group receiving the feedback improve, but often the students giving the feedback realize there's something they want to add or edit in their own project after viewing their peers' work. By incorporating opportunities to iterate based on feedback, teachers save themselves time and effort when marking the final product – as the product is invariably superior to what would have been submitted had the students not received formative feedback during the process.

Multiple attempts can be incorporated into a variety of assessment types to improve student learning outcomes. By allowing students to learn from their mistakes and revise their work, they can develop deeper understanding and mastery of the material.

Ensuring Fairness and Validity

WHEN I FIRST DECIDED to implement multiple attempts on assessments in my class, I was met with skepticism from some of my colleagues who believed that this would make it too easy for students to cheat or would give an unfair advantage to some students.

However, I firmly believe that with the right implementation and monitoring, multiple attempts can be done fairly and provide a valid representation of student learning. I set clear expectations for my students and emphasize the importance of taking each attempt seriously and using it as an opportunity to learn and improve.

Additionally, I carefully design my assessments to include a variety of question types and focus on assessing a range of skills and knowledge. This ensures that students cannot simply memorize answers from previous attempts but instead must demonstrate a true understanding of the material.

Through my use of multiple attempts, I have seen my students become more engaged and motivated to learn. They feel more confident in their abilities and are more willing to take risks and try new approaches. Overall, I believe that multiple attempts are a valuable tool for promoting student learning and ensuring fair and valid assessments.

Assessments play a critical role in education, and educators must ensure that the assessments they use are fair and valid measures of student learning. This chapter will discuss how to ensure the fairness and validity of assessments that utilize multiple attempts.

One of the concerns with multiple attempts assessments is that students who take the test multiple times may have an advantage over those who only take it once. To address this concern, there are two solutions. First, it is important to ensure that the questions and tasks in the assessment are consistent across attempts. This means that the assessment must be designed in a way that prevents students from memorizing the answers to specific questions. And second, it is essential to allow all students, regardless of their performance on the first assessment, to take the second if they so desire.

To ensure the validity of multiple attempts assessments, educators must consider the content and format of the assessment. The assessment should align with the learning objectives and curriculum standards. The tasks in the assessment should be designed to measure the desired learning outcomes. Additionally, the format of the assessment should be appropriate for the content being assessed. For example, multiple-choice questions may not be the best format for assessing a student's ability to write a persuasive essay.

It is also important to establish clear guidelines and criteria for how multiple attempts will be used in the assessment. This includes specifying the number of attempts that will be allowed, the time frame in which the attempts must be completed, and the consequences of each attempt. For example, the consequences of a second attempt may be different from the consequences of a first attempt.

Another consideration is the use of technology to facilitate multiple attempts assessments. Online platforms can make it easier for students to take assessments multiple times and receive immediate feedback. However, educators must be aware of the potential for cheating and take steps to prevent it, such as using different versions of the assessment for each attempt.

Overall, ensuring the fairness and validity of multiple attempts assessments requires careful planning and attention to detail. Educators must consider the content and format of the assessment, establish clear guidelines and criteria, and be aware of the potential challenges and benefits of using technology to facilitate multiple attempts. By doing so, they can create assessments that provide students with multiple opportunities to demonstrate their learning while maintaining the integrity of the assessment process.

Potential Road Blocks

AS A MIDDLE SCHOOL science teacher, I knew that allowing multiple attempts on assessments would benefit my students greatly. However, I also knew that there might be some pushback from parents and colleagues who were used to more traditional assessment methods. So, I decided to hold a parent-teacher conference night where I presented the research on the benefits of multiple attempts and how I planned to implement them in my classroom.

Some parents were initially skeptical, concerned that their children would rely too much on retakes and not learn the material thoroughly the first time. To address these concerns, I explained that students would still need to demonstrate a certain level of mastery on each assessment before moving on. The multiple attempts would give them the opportunity to practice and improve their understanding, but they would still need to show that they had learned the material in the end.

With colleagues, I presented data on how incorporating multiple attempts had increased student engagement, motivation, and performance in other classrooms. We discussed how multiple attempts could be implemented in a way that was fair and valid, and shared ideas on how to structure assessments to allow for multiple attempts.

By the end of the conference, most parents and colleagues were on board with the idea of multiple attempts. They appreciated the extra support it provided for students and the opportunity for them to improve their understanding of the material. And I was proud to have successfully advocated for a method that I knew would benefit my students in the long run.

Multiple attempts in assessments can be a controversial topic, and some educators and parents may have concerns about its effectiveness and practicality. In this chapter, we will explore some of the potential objections to multiple attempts and how they can be addressed.

Fear of Grade Inflation

One of the most common objections to multiple attempts is the fear that it will lead to grade inflation. Educators may worry that students will continue to retake assessments until they achieve the desired grade, regardless of their actual understanding of the material. However, this fear can be addressed by setting clear expectations for mastery and understanding. Students should be required to demonstrate a certain level of proficiency before moving on, rather than simply trying to achieve a high grade.

Concerns about Time and Resources

Another objection to multiple attempts is the concern that it may take up too much time and resources, particularly in larger classes. However, multiple attempts can actually save time in the long run by reducing the need for reteaching and remediation. Additionally, with the use of technology, assessments can be automatically graded and analyzed, reducing the workload for teachers.

Perceived Loss of Rigor

Some educators may worry that multiple attempts may lead to a perceived loss of rigor in the classroom. However, this objection can be addressed by emphasizing the importance of mastery and understanding, rather than simply achieving a high grade. By allowing students to demonstrate their understanding through multiple attempts, educators can promote a deeper and more meaningful understanding of the material.

Concerns about Fairness

Finally, some educators and parents may worry that multiple attempts may not be fair to all students, particularly those who may not have access to technology or other resources. This concern can be addressed by ensuring that all students have equal access to resources and support, and by designing assessments that are inclusive and equitable for all learners.

Food For Thought

Additionally, if the assessment is set up to truly assess student understanding, and the student takes the time and puts in the effort to learn the material, don't they deserve the grade? Ultimately, grades are supposed to be a reflection of student learning – if a student practices until they've mastered something, their grade should reflect that.

While there may be potential objections to multiple attempts in assessments, these concerns can be addressed through clear expectations, effective use of technology, and a focus on mastery and understanding rather than simply achieving a high grade. By allowing students to demonstrate their understanding through multiple attempts, educators can promote a deeper and more meaningful learning experience for all students.

Addressing Stakeholder Concerns

I HAD A STUDENT IN my grade 11 English class who struggled with anxiety during assessments. She was a hard-working student and always did her best, but her anxiety often got in the way of her success on exams. When I suggested offering multiple attempts on our next major essay, she was thrilled. Her mother, on the other hand, was not.

At parent-teacher conferences, her mother expressed her concerns about the multiple attempts policy. She argued that it would give some students an unfair advantage and would not accurately reflect their learning. I explained to her that multiple attempts were not about giving students an advantage, but rather about creating an opportunity for students to improve their understanding and skills.

I also shared with her how the essay assessments were structured, and how students were required to reflect on their mistakes and revise their work. I pointed out that by providing feedback and allowing for multiple attempts, I was actually fostering a more thorough understanding of the subject matter.

To my surprise, the mother actually thanked me for explaining the policy and reassured me that she would support her daughter in taking advantage of the multiple attempts. In the end, the policy worked out well for my student and many others, and it helped me to build stronger relationships with parents and guardians who may have initially been skeptical of the approach.

While multiple attempts for assessments have been shown to be beneficial for students, some teachers, students, and parents may have concerns about its implementation. In this chapter, we will address common concerns and provide solutions to overcome them.

Concern: *It will take too much time and effort for teachers to grade multiple attempts.*

Solution: There are various tools and resources available to make grading multiple attempts easier, such as automated grading systems, peer review, and rubrics. Additionally, the benefits of multiple attempts, such as improved learning outcomes and increased student engagement, can outweigh the extra time and effort needed for grading.

Concern: *Multiple attempts may lead to cheating and undermine the validity of assessments.*

Solution: To minimize the risk of cheating, teachers can use a variety of strategies, such as using randomized questions and answer choices, setting time limits, and using proctoring software. Teachers can also emphasize the importance of academic integrity and establish clear guidelines and consequences for cheating.

Concern: *Multiple attempts may give some students an unfair advantage over others.*

Solution: Teachers can ensure fairness by setting clear guidelines for the number of attempts and the time frame for completion. They can also provide different versions of the assessment or different questions to different students. Additionally, teachers can use a variety of assessment methods to ensure that students with different strengths and weaknesses have multiple opportunities to demonstrate their learning.

Concern: *Multiple attempts may discourage students from putting in their best effort on the first attempt.*

Solution: Teachers can address this concern by providing incentives for students to do their best on the first attempt, such as requiring students to give up their own personal time before school, at lunch, or after school to take subsequent attempts. Additionally, teachers can provide timely and constructive feedback to help students improve on subsequent attempts.

Food For Thought

A review, or practice version, of the assessment can eliminate many of these concerns while also providing all students with a fair and valid opportunity to learn from their mistakes before taking the graded version of the assessment.

Examples in Practice

I REMEMBER THE FIRST time I saw the results of multiple attempts being implemented in a colleague's classroom.

I had always been a bit skeptical of the concept, but seeing the way it transformed my colleague's classroom was truly inspiring. The students were engaged, motivated, and taking ownership of their own learning in a way I had never seen before. I could see the progress they were making, and it was clear that the multiple attempts were making a huge difference in their understanding of the material.

Seeing these results made me eager to try it out in my own classroom, and I'm so glad that I did. Multiple attempts have become a regular part of my assessments, and I can confidently say that it has made a positive impact on my students' learning and growth.

Multiple attempts in assessments can benefit students by giving them the opportunity to demonstrate their learning over time and improve their scores. However, some teachers and educators may have concerns about the practicality and fairness of multiple attempts. This chapter will provide real-life examples of successful implementation of multiple attempts in classrooms and address some of the common concerns and challenges.

One example of successful implementation of multiple attempts is the use of retake policies in high school math classes. Teachers who have implemented retake policies have reported positive outcomes, including increased student engagement and motivation, higher student achievement, and improved student attitudes towards math. In these classrooms, students are given multiple attempts to demonstrate their understanding of the material, and their final grade is based on their highest score. This approach has been found to encourage students to take risks and to seek feedback from their teachers, resulting in improved learning outcomes.

Another example of successful implementation of multiple attempts is the use of formative assessments in elementary schools. Formative assessments are designed to provide ongoing feedback to students and teachers, allowing them to adjust instruction and learning strategies to better meet the needs of individual students. By giving students multiple attempts to complete formative assessments, teachers can provide targeted feedback and support to help students achieve success. This approach has been found to promote deeper learning and to help students develop a growth mindset, as they see the value of feedback and understand that mistakes are an opportunity for learning.

A third example of successful implementation of multiple attempts is the use of project-based assessments in middle and high school social studies classes. In these assessments, students are given a task or project that requires them to demonstrate their understanding of key concepts and skills. Students are given multiple opportunities to revise and refine their work, based on feedback from teachers and peers, before submitting a final product. This approach has been found to promote critical thinking and collaboration, as well as to improve student motivation and engagement.

While multiple attempts in assessments can provide many benefits for students, there may be concerns about the validity and fairness of the approach. For example, some teachers may worry that giving students multiple attempts may lead to grade inflation or may not accurately reflect students' true understanding of the material. However, these concerns can be addressed through careful design of assessments and by providing clear guidelines and expectations for multiple attempts.

Food For Thought

If students are genuinely learning the content, is grade inflation even a thing? If students simply repeat the exact same test until they've memorized the correct answers, that would inflate grades. However, if students are taking different versions of the assessments, or making changes to projects based on feedback, they're learning and engaging with the material more deeply and in a more meaningful manner. This isn't grade inflation – it's effective teaching. It means more students are learning the content at a higher level. Ultimately, it proves the teacher has done a better job of helping all students work toward mastery and makes the grades more meaningful, not less so.

Final Thoughts

I'VE BEEN TEACHING in the classroom for fifteen years, and I've seen the incredible impact that multiple attempts can have on student learning. I remember the moment the power of multiple assessments really sank in for me. I had one student in particular who struggled with a difficult math concept. She failed the traditional assessment, but with the option of multiple attempts, she was able to revisit the material and try again. On her second attempt, she showed significant improvement and finally grasped the concept.

That experience showed me just how much power there is in giving students the opportunity to learn from their mistakes and try again. It's not just about getting a passing grade, but about promoting deeper understanding and long-term retention of knowledge. And it's not just for struggling students either – even my high-achieving students have benefited from the chance to perfect their understanding through multiple attempts.

Overall, multiple attempts on assessments have proven to be a powerful tool for student learning and growth. It's time for more educators to recognize this and incorporate multiple attempts into their own teaching practices.

As we've seen throughout this book, providing students with multiple opportunities to demonstrate their understanding is a powerful tool for enhancing learning outcomes. Whether it's through offering multiple attempts on a quiz or exam, providing opportunities for revision and feedback, or implementing project-based assessments that allow for multiple paths to success, giving students the chance to try again and again is an effective way to promote mastery, retention, and overall academic success.

The benefits of multiple attempts are clear: students are able to learn from their mistakes, identify areas where they need improvement, and build the confidence and skills necessary to tackle challenging academic tasks. Moreover, this approach benefits students of all skill levels, from struggling learners who need extra support and practice to advanced students who want to deepen their understanding and explore more complex ideas.

Of course, implementing multiple attempts in assessments is not without its challenges. Educators must be intentional about designing assessments that are fair, valid, and aligned with their learning objectives. They must also be prepared to address concerns from students, parents, and colleagues who may be resistant to this approach.

However, with the right strategies and support, it is possible to successfully integrate multiple attempts into your teaching and assessment practices. By doing so, you will not only enhance the learning outcomes of your students, but also create a more inclusive and equitable classroom environment that values growth, persistence, and resilience.

In conclusion, the importance of multiple attempts in assessments cannot be overstated. As educators, we have the responsibility to provide our students with the tools, resources, and opportunities they need to succeed academically and beyond. By embracing a growth mindset and implementing multiple attempts in our teaching and assessment practices, we can help our students reach their full potential and achieve their goals.

Call to Action

AS A TEACHER WHO HAS seen the benefits of multiple attempts on assessments firsthand, I encourage my fellow educators to consider implementing this practice in their own classrooms. By allowing students the opportunity to learn from their mistakes and improve their understanding, we can foster a growth mindset and promote long-term retention of knowledge.

I understand that there may be concerns about fairness and validity of assessments, but by carefully designing assessments and providing appropriate feedback, we can ensure that multiple attempts are done fairly and provide a valid representation of student learning.

I challenge my fellow educators to think critically about their assessment practices and consider incorporating multiple attempts to promote a culture of learning and growth in their classrooms. Together, we can create a more equitable and effective learning environment for all students.

As educators, we have the responsibility to provide fair and meaningful assessments that accurately measure student learning. Traditional assessment methods have been the norm for many years, but they come with limitations and disadvantages that can negatively impact students' success. In this book, we have explored the benefits of providing multiple attempts for assessments, and now it's time to take action and implement these strategies in our own classrooms.

By implementing multiple attempts in your assessments, you are providing your students with a fair and meaningful assessment experience. You are also promoting a growth mindset that encourages students to see mistakes as opportunities for learning and improvement. It may take some time to adjust to this new approach, but the benefits will be worth it for both you and your students.

We must move away from traditional assessment methods and embrace new strategies that promote student success. Multiple attempts are a powerful tool that can benefit students of all skill levels and ensure fairness in assessment. It is up to us as educators to take action and implement these strategies in our own classrooms to create a more equitable and effective learning environment.

Resources and Tools

IMPLEMENTING MULTIPLE attempts in assessments is a beneficial practice for student learning, but it is also a challenging one for educators. In this section, we will explore some resources and tools that can help educators effectively implement multiple attempts in assessments.

Digital Assessment Platforms

One of the easiest ways to implement multiple attempts in assessments is by using digital assessment platforms. These platforms, such as Microsoft or Google Forms, Quizlet, Kahoot, and Edpuzzle, allow educators to create assessments with multiple attempts and provide instant feedback to students.

Formative Assessment Tools

Formative assessment tools, such as Socrative, Nearpod, and Mentimeter, allow educators to create interactive assessments that can be used for pre-assessment, practice, and post-assessment. These tools provide instant feedback to students and allow educators to identify areas where students need additional support.

Rubrics

Rubrics can be a useful tool for implementing multiple attempts in assessments. By providing students with clear grading criteria and feedback, educators can give students the opportunity to improve their work and attempt the assessment multiple times.

Differentiated Instruction Strategies

Differentiated instruction strategies, such as tiered assignments, can provide students with multiple opportunities to demonstrate their understanding of a topic. By offering different levels of complexity in assignments, educators can cater to the needs of all students and provide opportunities for students to attempt the assessment multiple times.

Collaborative Learning Strategies

Collaborative learning strategies, such as group projects and peer feedback, can provide students with multiple opportunities to learn and demonstrate their understanding of a topic. By working in groups and providing feedback to each other, students can learn from their mistakes and improve their understanding of the topic.

Professional Development Opportunities

Professional development opportunities can help educators learn how to effectively implement multiple attempts in assessments. Workshops, conferences, and online courses can provide educators with the knowledge and skills necessary to implement multiple attempts in assessments and support student learning.

Further Reading

BROOKHART, SUSAN M. and Thomas R. Guskey, editors. *What We Know About Grading: What Works, What Doesn't, and What's Next.* ASCD, 2019.

Dueck, Myron. *Grading Smarter, Not Harder: Assessment Strategies That Motivate Kids and Help Them Learn.* ASCD, 2014.

Feldman, Joe. *Grading for Equity: What It Is, Why It Matters, and How It Can Transform Schools and Classrooms.* SAGE Publications, 2018.

Wexler, Natalie. *The Knowledge Gap: The Hidden Cause of America's Broken Education System—and How to Fix it*. Penguin Publishing Group, 2020.

Wormeli, Rick. *Fair Isn't Always Equal: Assessing & Grading in the Differentiated Classroom*. Stenhouse Publishers, 2006.

Don't miss out!

Visit the website below and you can sign up to receive emails whenever Cheryl Angst publishes a new book. There's no charge and no obligation.

https://books2read.com/r/B-A-SBAY-AMMIC

BOOKS 2 READ

Connecting independent readers to independent writers.

About the Author

Cheryl Angst has been teaching in the classroom for over twenty-five years. With a Masters in curriculum and instruction, her passion centers around finding tips, tricks, and strategies to enhance her practice.

Cheryl is a firm believer that learning should be fun for both the students and the teacher. If it isn't engaging, or doesn't spark joy, it's likely able to be done differently.

The "Quick Reads for Busy Educators" series is designed to maximize the precious time educators have. Each book is short enough to be read in an hour or less, but contains a wealth of information on the topic. Some books are overviews of strategies and approaches (enough to help educators decide if it's for them) and some are deeper dives into specific aspects of those larger approaches. This allows busy educators to grab the information they need quickly and efficiently.

If there's a topic you'd like to see covered in the "Quick Reads" series, please let us know!

www.ingramcontent.com/pod-product-compliance
Lightning Source LLC
Chambersburg PA
CBHW070317160726
47999CB00003B/1064